DISCOVER!

I0876247

EARTH AND SPACE
SCIENCE

CELESTIAL OBJECTS

Beth Irving

Enslow PUBLISHING

Please visit our website, www.enslow.com. For a free color catalog of all our high-quality books, call toll free 1-800-398-2504 or fax 1-877-980-4454.

Cataloging-in-Publication Data
Names: Irving, Beth.
Title: Celestial objects / Beth Irving.
Description: Buffalo, NY : Enslow Publishing, 2027. | Series: Earth and space science | Includes glossary and index.
Identifiers: ISBN 9781978550230 (pbk.) | ISBN 9781978550247 (library bound) | ISBN 9781978550254 (ebook)
Subjects: LCSH: Astronomy–Juvenile literature. | Sky–Juvenile literature. | Constellations–Juvenile literature.
Classification: LCC QB46.I785 2027 | DDC 520–dc23

Published in 2027 by
Enslow Publishing
2544 Clinton Street
Buffalo, NY 14224

Copyright © 2027 Enslow Publishing

Designer: Claire Vanden Branden
Editor: Noah Riccardi

Photo Credits: Cover, p. 1 Ikunl/Shutterstock.com; p. 5 twabian/Shutterstock.com; p. 7 Goinyk Production/Shutterstock.com; p. 9 Withan Tor/Shutterstock.com; p. 10 Feng Cheng/Shutterstock.com; p. 11 Vadim Sadovski/Shutterstock.com; p. 13 djgis/Shutterstock.com; p. 15 Kubilay Archive/Shutterstock.com; p. 17 Johann Weitweg/Shutterstock.com; p. 19 AstroStar/Shutterstock.com; p. 21 Dima Zel/Shutterstock.com.

All rights reserved. No part of this book may be reproduced in any form without permission in writing from the publisher, except by a reviewer.

Printed in China

CPSIA compliance information: Batch #QS27ENS: For further information contact Enslow Publishing, at 1-800-398-2504.

Find us on

CONTENTS

WHAT'S IN THE SKY 4
THE SOLAR SYSTEM 8
SUN AND MOON 12
THE NIGHT SKY 16
LOOKING UP 18
GLOSSARY 22
FOR MORE INFORMATION 23
INDEX 24

BOLDFACE WORDS APPEAR IN THE GLOSSARY.

WHAT'S IN THE SKY

Have you ever looked up into the sky? There are lots of cool things to see. The sky doesn't look the same in the day as it does at night.

During the day, the sky appears light blue. We can see the sun and clouds. At night, the sky appears much darker. We can see stars and the moon.

The Earth is always spinning. The sky seems to change because Earth faces different directions. The objects in the sky don't actually change. The things we can see from our spot on Earth change.

Most things we see in the sky are very far away. These **celestial** objects are in outer space. Outer space is huge.

THE SOLAR SYSTEM

Earth is in the solar system. It's like an outer space **neighborhood**. Our solar system has eight planets. Earth is one of those planets.

We can see Mars from Earth. Mars is red. This makes it look different from all the other planets in our solar system. Mars appears very bright at nighttime.

The easiest planet to see from Earth is Venus. Venus is the brightest planet in the night sky. When we see it, it can look white or even a little bit blue.

In the photo on page 10, Venus is the white dot above and to the right of the moon.

SUN AND MOON

The sun and the moon are in the sky, too. The sun is big and very hot. Did you know that the sun is a star?

The sun comes up in the morning. This is called a sunrise. At night, the sun goes away. This is called a sunset. This happens because Earth is spinning.

The sun is always shining onto the moon. At night, we see the moon because it **reflects** light from the sun onto Earth. This is why the moon shines at night.

The moon looks different on different days of the month. That's because it **orbits** around the Earth. The moon takes about one month to make one full orbit.

THE NIGHT SKY

Stars make the night sky look pretty. Sometimes, we see **constellations**. Constellations are shapes made of stars. The Big Dipper is a constellation.

A long time ago, people used the stars to guide them. The stars helped people figure out directions when they were in new places.

LOOKING UP

We can see some of the night sky with just our eyes. Tools can help us see even more stuff. One tool we use is a **telescope**.

Telescopes help us see things that are really far away. They help us see things we couldn't see with just our eyes.

Some people have a telescope in their backyard. They look up into the night sky for fun. There's a lot to find in the sky!

Some big telescopes float in space. They take pictures of planets and stars that we can't see from the ground. It's fun to look at the sky. We can spot new things every day. What things do you see in the sky?

GLOSSARY

celestial: In the sky or outer space.

constellations: Groups of stars that form figures.

neighborhood: An area of things close to one another.

orbits: Moves in a circle around something. Also, the path of an object that moves in a circle around another object.

reflects: Sends back light.

telescope: A tool used to see things that are far away.

FOR MORE INFORMATION

Books

Andrews, Elizabeth. *Planets*. Minneapolis, MN: Abdo Publishing, 2025.

Miller, Ron. *To the Stars: The Story of NASA*. Minneapolis, MN: Lerner Publications, 2026.

Websites

Britannica Kids: Astronomy
kids.britannica.com/kids/article/astronomy/352798
Learn more about astronomy, the study of outer space.

National Geographic Kids: Passport to Space
kids.nationalgeographic.com/space
Learn more about outer space at this website.

Publisher's note to educators and parents: Our editors have carefully reviewed these websites to ensure that they are suitable for students. Many websites change frequently, however, and we cannot guarantee that a site's future contents will continue to meet our high standards of quality and educational value. Be advised that students should be closely supervised whenever they access the internet.

INDEX

clouds, 4
constellations, 16
days, 4, 14, 20
Earth, 6, 8, 10, 12, 14
Mars, 8
moon, 4, 10, 12, 14
night, 4, 10, 12, 14, 18, 20
outer space, 6, 8
planets, 8, 10, 20
solar system, 8
stars, 4, 12, 16, 20
sun, 4, 12, 14
telescopes, 18, 20
Venus, 10